NATIONAL GEOGRAPHIC

T0045529

Who Works on the Beach?

Claude Wright

I work on the beach.
I sell ice cream and drinks.
I help people cool off.

I work on the beach.
I pick up trash left on the sand.
I help keep the beach clean and safe.

I work on the beach.
I watch the swimmers.
I help people stay safe in the water.

I work on the beach.
I rent sailboats.
I help people sail on the sea.

7618
RAPID

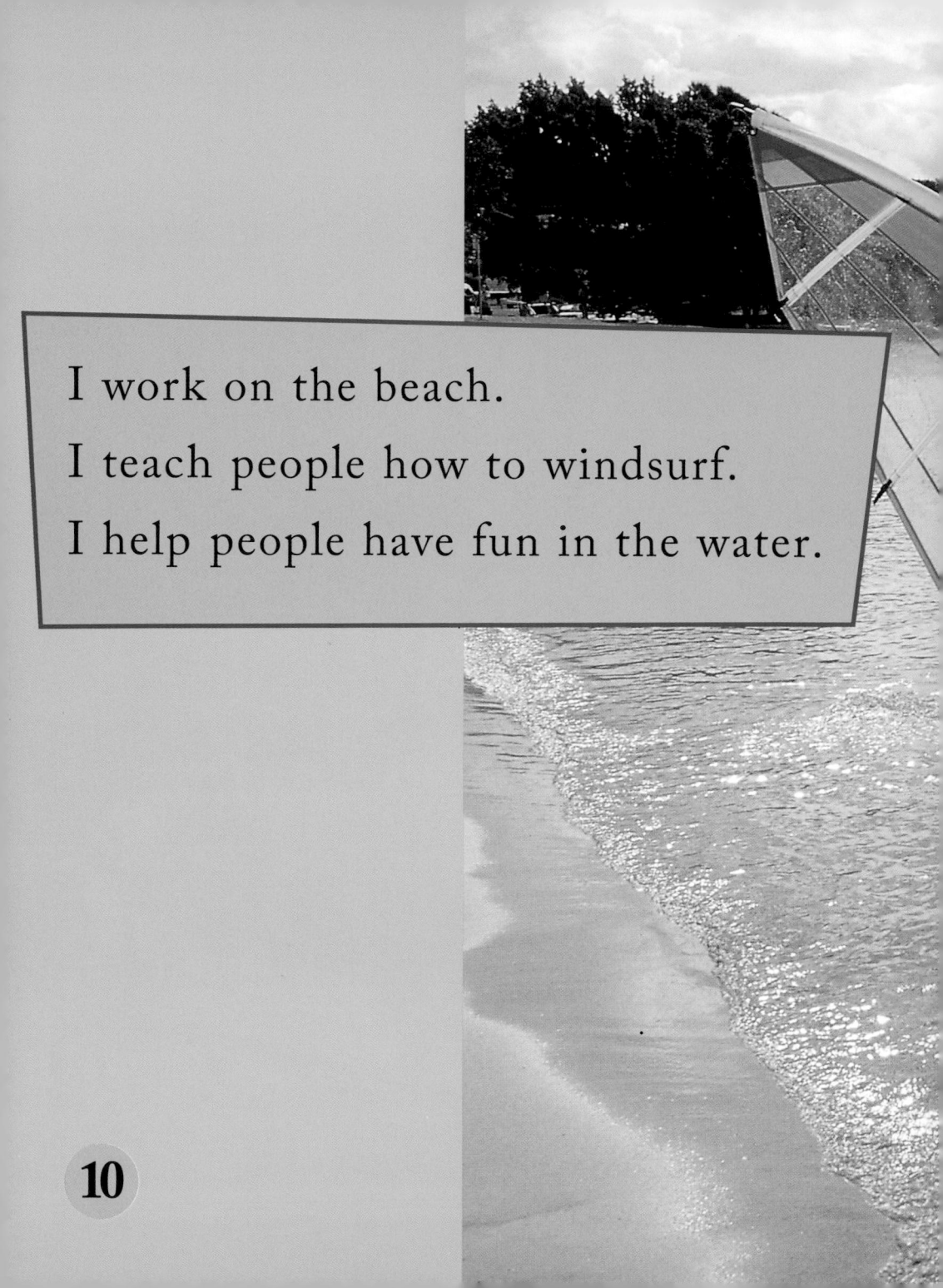

I work on the beach.
I teach people how to windsurf.
I help people have fun in the water.

Many people work on the beach.
They make it a fun place to visit.